A KID'S GUIDE TO

Chicago

Photography by Don Brown

Written by Karen T. Bartlett

First published in the United States
of America by:

Twin Lights Publishers, Inc.
8 Hale Street
Rockport, Massachusetts 01966
Telephone: (978) 546-7398
http://www.twinlightspub.com

ISBN: 978-1-934907-03-0
ISBN: 1-934907-03-0

10 9 8 7 6 5 4 3 2

Painting of the Pioneer Zephyr
on page 61 used with permission
of artist Mike Danneman. Visit
www.railroademporium.com to
purchase a copy of this painting.

Book design by
SYP Design & Production, Inc.
http://www.sypdesign.com

Printed in China

*i*f you're looking for a boring old grownup guidebook, skip this book! *A Kid's Guide to Chicago* is a lively and deliciously different view of one of the most exciting cities in America.

Designed with pre-schoolers to young teens in mind, this book reveals what kids really want to know: What is that bizarre green gunk on a Chicago hot dog? Who put the Billy Goat Curse on the Chicago Cubs? What's the true scoop on Mrs. O'Leary's cow?

In simple dictionary style, packed with over 100 colorful pictures by talented photographer Don Brown, this soft-cover treasure showcases Chicago from A to Z. Kids will discover awesome stuff, like where to see a hairy tarantula as big as a Chicago pizza, sculptures of 100 headless people, and Abraham Lincoln's death bed. They'll find out how to meet Staley da Bear, mascot for the Chicago Bears, where to get their picture taken in front of a 101-foot baseball bat, and where they can dig up dinosaur bones or feed a butterfly.

Whether they're budding nuclear physicists, brain surgeons, or plan to follow in basketball superstar Michael Jordan's footsteps, Chicago has an activity or attraction to wow them.

A Kid's Guide to Chicago is a fun way to learn about the Great Fire of 1871, Chicago's World's Fairs, the story of Juicy Fruit Gum and more.

The following 60 pages reveal scores of attractions from the Holocaust Museum to Legoland® to the International Museum of Surgical Science, as well as spectacular buildings, beautiful public spaces, and lots of cool things to do for free.

Parents and grandparents, teachers and armchair travelers will all appreciate the generous coverage of this city's history, geography, art, music, and culture. Kids and grownups alike are sure to ooh and aah, and laugh out loud as gifted writer Karen T. Bartlett takes them on a super-size Chicago adventure, with fascinating stories, quirky factoids, and a generous helping of silliness.

Ablaze!

The Great Chicago Fire of 1871: Was Mrs. O'Leary's cow guilty?

There are many stories and even a song about a cow that kicked over a lantern in the O'Leary barn and set the hay on fire. They said that the barn burned down, then the famous wind that blows through the city sent flames to other buildings. Soon, the whole city was on fire. Since most buildings were wood, the whole city was destroyed. Nobody is sure how the fire really started, but one thing is true: every Chicagoan knows the time and date: 9 P.M., October 8, 1871.

Absolutely Awesome World's Fairs: 1893 and 1933.

When something has more than one name it can get totally confusing. So here's the scoop on Chicago's two World's Fairs. They're not really called the Absolutely Awesome World's Fairs (so don't ever write that name on a test!) but here's an easy way to remember which was which: Each one had a special color, and each one had its own spectacular fair ride.

Absolutely Awesome World's Fair #1 — 1893.

Real name: World's Columbian Exposition.

The first fair celebrated the 400th anniversary of Christopher Columbus' landing in the New World. The city was 60 years old then, but really it was only 22, because it had to start over after the Great Fire of 1871. Its buildings were white, so it was called the White City. Its spectacular fair ride was the Ferris Wheel that you can see on page 17. More than 20 million people visited the fair.

Absolutely Awesome World's Fair #2 — 1933.

Real name: Century of Progress Exposition.

The second fair was Chicago's 100th birthday party, and more than 30 million people came to see what the future might be like. One of the most exciting exhibits was the *House of Tomorrow*. The buildings of this fair were painted in bright colors, so it was called the Rainbow City. Its spectacular ride was the Sky Ride, with rocket-shaped cars for people to ride from one end of the fair to the other.

Adler Planetarium & Astronomy Museum: Black holes, aliens and more.

For anyone who loves stars, planets and constellations, and anyone curious about black holes, space and even aliens, this is an excellent place to spend the day. Besides the largest telescope in the Midwest, it has shows and exhibits for everyone from pre-schoolers to grownups.

Agora: 100 headless people.

None of the bronze people in this picture have heads. Or arms, either. The bodies look kind of like tree trunks, don't they? Which is cool, because the main part of a person's body is called a trunk. You can see this forest of people at Grant Park. The sculptor named this forest *Agora*, which is a Greek word for "gathering place."

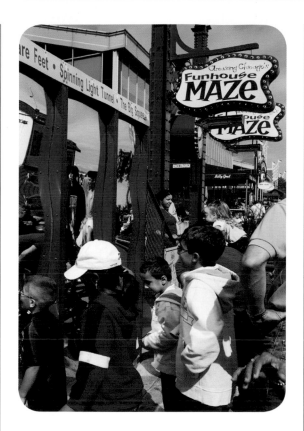

Amazing Chicago's Funhouse Maze: You'll laugh your head off.

This is a crazy fun place on the Navy Pier. You can go through the *Rainbow Tunnel*, the *Elevator Drop*, the *Big Squeeze* and the *Mirror Maze*, and then head over to the *Psychedelic Mine Shaft* and the *Spinning Tunnel*. Stomp, spin, bounce, and get dizzy – and then do it all again!

Aquarium! Pet a penguin – or be one!

What would you do if a beluga whale crinkled its melon at you? You'd laugh, we bet, because "melon" is whale-talk for "forehead." Baby belugas also whistle and spit. You can see them, and a gazillion other sea and land creatures, at the John G. Shedd Aquarium. How about a hairy tarantula as big as a 12-inch pizza? Or an orange-spotted, horned dragon moray eel, covered with slimy mucus? Eeeeew! Little kids can put on penguin suits and see what it's like to be one. Kids and grownups of all ages absolutely, positively must see the new live sea show, *Fantasea*. It has actors in costume, animation and virtual reality. The Shedd Aquarium is on the Museum Campus on Lakeshore Drive.

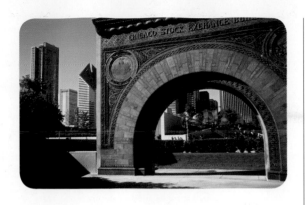

Arch
Hey, where's the building?

This is a very impressive front door, isn't it? But what happened to the rest of the building? Well, there was a huge building, a long time ago. It was the Chicago Stock Exchange – but it wasn't really here in this lovely garden. It was torn down to build a new one, but this arch was just too beautiful to tear down, so it was carefully moved here, to the Art Institute of Chicago.

Art Institute of Chicago
Lions are standing guard.

Imagine 300,000 paintings, statues and all kinds of other art in one place! Before you go inside, be sure to get your picture taken in front of one of the huge bronze lions that stand guard in front. Inside, one of our favorite exhibits is *BIGsmall*, where small things get big and big things get small, and other magical things can happen.

BP Pedestrian Bridge

Is it a sheet metal snake or the coolest bridge in Chicago? It's both, kind of. This amazing, curving, slithering bridge crosses Columbus Drive, so people can walk from Millennium Park to the Daley Bicentennial Plaza sports complex.

Baboon? Decide for yourself!

It's 50 feet tall, weighs 162 tons, and some people say it looks like a baboon. Who made it? Pablo Picasso, one of the most famous artists in the history of the world. But here's the interesting thing: he didn't give this sculpture a name like he usually did. Some people think he was making fun of Chicago by giving them a baboon. Go to Daley Plaza and check it out for yourself.

Balbo Monument: A 2,000 year-old temple column.

A very surprising thing to find in the center of Chicago, isn't it? This column is from the ruins of an ancient Roman temple. It was a present to this city, brought all the way from Italy to celebrate the first Italian Air Force flight across the Atlantic Ocean. It was displayed at Awesome World's Fair #2, and now stands on a pedestal in Burnham Park.

Batcolumn: A 101-foot-tall baseball bat.

A famous Swedish sculptor named Claes Oldenburg likes to make really gigantic sculptures. People love his giant-size ice cream cone, giant cowboy hats, and giant toothbrush with giant toothpaste to match. Chicago has his giant baseball bat, as tall as a 10-story building. It stands outside the Social Security Administration Building.

Batman Returns
Hey, that's our bridge!

In the movie *Batman Returns*, the bridge that connects The Narrows to Gotham City is Chicago's very own Franklin Bridge! Many scenes for *Batman, Spider-Man* and other movies were filmed in Chicago.

The Bean: Liquid mercury and steel.

It might be the biggest bean you have ever seen in your life. Its called Cloud Gate, and you'll find it in the AT&T Plaza of Millennium Park. It is 66 feet long, 33 feet high, and weighs over 110 tons. They call it "The Bean" because that's what it looks like. Walk all around it (under it too) to see the city of Chicago reflected like a mirror.

Bears!
The Chicago Bears football team, that is.

Chicago loves its football team, the Bears, winners of Super Bowl XX. Their colors are orange and navy, and their mascot is Staley Da Bear. They play their home games at Soldier Field.

Billy Goat Curse
A very funny baseball story.

When William Sianis got kicked out of the baseball stadium for bringing his stinky goat to a World Series game, he was so mad he said he was putting a curse on the home team, the Chicago Cubs. He said the Cubs would never win a pennant or go to the World Series. Most people don't really believe in curses, but it sure seems so sometimes, because so far the Cubs have not won a pennant or made it to the World Series.

Blackhawks®
Nope, not birds — it's Chicago's pro hockey team.

The Chicago Blackhawks® must not have a curse on them, because they have won thirteen divisional titles and three Stanley Cup® championships. They play their home games at the United Center. One of their sponsors is Chicago's famous bright yellow Lemonhead candy.

Blue Angels
Best air show of the summer.

Their real name is the U.S. Navy Flight Demonstration Squadron, but everybody calls these daring Navy and Marine Corps pilots the Blue Angels. Their air shows are so exciting that sometimes you have to remind yourself to breathe. The Blue Angels perform every August at the huge Chicago Air and Water Show. Besides the buzzing and booming of fighter jets flying up to 700 miles per hour, there are military parachute demonstrations, amazing water skiing and boat-jumping tricks, and lots more.

Blues Festival

The saying "singing the blues" started in the days of slavery when life was hard. People sang songs about their problems. Every summer, nearly a million people come to the Chicago Blues Festival in Grant Park to hear the best blues musicians in the world. The concert goes on for three days!

Bowman and Spearman: Native American warriors.

What do you notice about this statue of a great warrior on horseback? It looks like he is shooting an arrow, but there is no bow and no arrow! There's another warrior on horseback too, and he looks like he's throwing a spear. But there is no spear! It's a mystery why Ivan Mestrovic, the sculptor, decided to leave out the weapons. Check out these great bronze statues in Grant Park.

Bulls
Pro basketball superstars.

Michael Jordan, the greatest basketball player of all time, was a member of the Chicago Bulls. Their home games are played in the United Center. Their colors are red and black and their mascot is Benny the Bull. They wear black shoes and black socks during playoff games. One time, they decided not to wear black — and they lost. "Air Jordan," #23, retired in 1999. Read more about him on page 27.

Burnham, Daniel
He drew up the Plan of Chicago.

This famous architect did such a great job designing Awesome World's Fair #1 that the city of Chicago hired him to make a modern new design for the city. That made him one of America's first "urban planners." He believed in big ideas, and he once said in a speech, "Make no small plans. They have no magic to stir men's blood."

Butterfly Haven: 1,000 butterflies.

If you've never had a chance to get up close to a shimmering blue butterfly as big as a parakeet, go straight to The Judy Istock Butterfly Haven at the Peggy Notebaert Nature Museum! The spectacular Blue Morpho butterfly is from the South American rainforest. It's one of 75 different species from around the world that flit around and rest on flowers just inches away from you. In the lab, you can watch caterpillars make cocoons and maybe see a butterfly hatch.

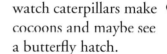

C

Century of Progress Exposition

Which Awesome World's Fair was this? What color was the city? What was the famous fair ride? Go back to page 4 to find out!

Chicago Cultural Center
Performances! Films! Workshops! Celebrations! All free!

Besides free music, dance and family events, the Chicago Cultural Center is an architectural showcase. Check out the world's largest Tiffany art glass dome, made of 30,000 pieces of colorful glass. It's worth more than 35 million dollars!

Chicago Harbor Lighthouse:
Protecting ships since 1919.

The pretty red and white lighthouse with the cone-shaped tower was built for Awesome World's Fair #1. It still sends its beam out to ships as far as 24 miles away, and guides them into the harbor. You can get a great view of it from the Navy Pier.

Chicago History Museum
Stuff you can't see or do anyplace else in the world.

You can ride a high-wheel bicycle down a wood-paved street, see President Abraham Lincoln's deathbed, hear the roar of the Great Chicago Fire, build a bridge, or catch a fly ball at Comiskey Park. And yes, you can be a Chicago style-hot dog. Don't believe it? Get your free Great Kids Museum Passport at any Chicago public library and go see for yourself.

Chicago Theatre: A royal palace.

People once called this seven-story building the "Wonder Theatre of the World," because it was the first movie theater in America built like a royal palace. Check out the grand staircase and the ceiling murals. The beautiful arch looks like the famous Arc de Triomphe in Paris. They don't show movies here anymore, but it's fun to dress up to see a play or show onstage at the Chicago Theatre.

Chicago Public Library

After the Great Fire of 1871, the people of Chicago wanted to start a library. They decided that since the city water tank did not burn down in the fire, it would be a safe, fireproof location. Since that first water tank, the library has grown to 79 locations and more than ten million books. If you go to the main branch, don't forget to look up! There's a green gargoyle on the roof!

Chicago River
Yes, it really flows backwards!

The 156 mile-long river used to flow from west to east into Lake Michigan, but sewage was being dumped into the lake and ruining the drinking water. So, some very smart engineers designed a lock system that directs the flow in the opposite direction. If you're here on St. Patrick's Day, don't be surprised to see that the river has been dyed green. It's green in an eco-way too, because the dye is safe for fish and wildlife.

Chicagoan: If you were born in Chicago, or live here now, that's you!

Here's how you say it: "Chicago-un."

Chicago's Harbors: 5,000 Boats.

The string of nine harbors along Chicago's waterfront is the largest harbor system in America. If you happen to be traveling around on your yacht, you can sail right up to many of the attractions in this book! If not, check out the water taxi on page 55.

Children's Museum: A place of wonder at the Navy Pier.

If you always wanted to invent something, Chicago Children's Museum is the place to do it. It has all the stuff imaginable to build a flying machine or crazy gadget. Would you rather dig for dinosaur bones or climb the masts to the top of a ship? Or be a firefighter, or explore the bottom of the ocean? All of that? No problem! The museum isn't just for looking, it's for doing. Even grownup kids have a blast here.

Chinatown

Chicago is lucky to have a large community of Chinese heritage. If you aren't planning a trip to China this year, no problem! Just visit Chinatown on Chicago's South Side, with its real Chinese restaurants and shops. Have your picture taken beneath the beautiful red Chinatown Gate. If you're here during the Chinese New Year, there's a great parade. And be sure to touch the Nine Dragon Wall for good luck.

Christopher Columbus Statues
Honoring Chicago's Italian heritage.

The Italian-American people of Chicago donated this statue by Carlo Brioschi to the city for Awesome World's Fair #2. You can see it in Grant Park. Can you find other Columbus statues around town? Hint: Look for a nine-foot-tall bronze one in Columbus Memorial Plaza in the Little Italy neighborhood.

CityPASS
Show this to the grownups!

If you're planning to see several of Chicago's most famous attractions, you will definitely want a Chicago CityPASS. It will get you into seriously excellent places like the Adler Planetarium, the Museum of Science and Industry, the Aquarium and more, for almost half price. You can check it out online at www.citypass.com.

Clarence Buckingham Memorial Fountain
Shooting water and light show.

Imagine colorful jets of water shooting from this spectacular fountain, 150 feet into the sky. It happens every night, once every hour for 20 minutes from April to October. The splashy fountain is in the center of Grant Park. It was a gift to the city by a generous Chicagoan, Kate Buckingham, in memory of her brother, Clarence. The four seahorses at the base of the fountain symbolize the four states that touch Lake Michigan. Can you name them? Hint: One starts with the letter W, one starts with the letter M, and two start with the letter I.

Conservatories: Gardens under glass.

On a cold winter day, Chicago's conservatories seem like paradise with their orchids, ferns and bizarre tropical plants. Both the Lincoln Park Conservatory (here) and its sister, the Garfield Park Conservatory (on page 22) grow plants for the parks around Chicago. Admission is free.

Corn Cobs. But not really.

Many people think these two 60-story towers at Marina City look like ears of corn, so that's what they call them. Now, if someone tells you they live in a corn cob, you'll know what they are talking about.

Cow, Mrs. O'Leary's

That poor creature got blamed for something really, really bad. Find out what it was on page 4.

Crown Fountain:
Faces on a 50-foot tower

Is it a sculpture? A fountain? A giant video screen? Yes, all of these! The crazy-cool glass block towers in Millennium Park show giant pictures of real peoples' faces (maybe even yours). The fountain is set up so it looks like the people have water spouting from their mouths. Some grown-ups like it and some don't – but just about every kid in the universe does.

CTA: Two million riders every single day.

Try to wrap your brain around these numbers from the Chicago Transit Authority: The city buses make 24,000 trips a day and there are 144 train stations helping two million riders get around town. Imagine if all those people were driving cars! The Chicago Transit Authority is the second largest transit agency in the United States. Thanks, CTA, for helping to save the planet!

Cubbies

That's the nickname that Chicago Cubs baseball fans call their team. Their colors are red, white and blue. You can catch a Cubbies game at Wrigley Field. A long time ago the Cubs were called the Chicago White Stockings, but then that name went to another baseball team. Find out which one on page 56.

Daphne: A goddess or a tree?

Many Ancient Greek myths tell about a goddess named Daphne. Some say she was being chased by the god Apollo, so her mother changed her into a laurel tree to hide her. Dessa Kirk loves those stories, so she has made many Daphne sculptures. The Daphne Garden is at the corner of Roosevelt and Michigan Avenue.

Douglas, Stephen: He beat Abraham Lincoln for the Senate in 1858.

Of course, three years later Mr. Lincoln was elected president of the United States, so it worked out just fine. Senator Douglas proposed the Kansas-Nebraska Act, which let those territories decide for themselves whether or not to allow slavery. Mr. Douglas is buried in this impressive mausoleum with his statue on top.

DuSable, Jean Baptiste Pointe: Founder of Chicago.

This French/African trapper journeyed to the New World from Haiti to open a trading post around 1779. He became Chicago's first settler. Many places around town are named for him – a harbor, a school, even a dog park – but we think

the DuSable Museum of African American History is the most exciting. You can explore the continent of Africa, "meet" the first African-American soldiers, and come to an African American festival. It costs just one dollar for kids age 6 to 12, and on Sundays you can get in free.

Elks National Veterans Memorial
What a magnificent building this is!

The Benevolent and Protective Order of Elks of the United States of America (that's their whole name) has a million members. Their slogan is, "Elks Care and Elks Share." The Elks especially help children, and the men and women who have fought in America's wars. They built this memorial in Chicago to honor their one thousand members who died for their country in World War I.

Ferris Wheel
How did it get such a funny name?

The Ferris Wheel was invented by a man named George W. Ferris, so he got to name it after himself. He showed it at Awesome World's Fair #1. Back then, a 20-minute ride cost 50 cents. The one you can ride at the Navy Pier is exactly like it. It now costs $6 and only lasts 7 minutes… but wait till you see the view of the city from way up there!

Field Museum of Natural History: Biggest Tyrannosaurus Rex on the planet.

How would you like to travel through four billion years on earth, from before the time of dinosaurs? You can, at the Field Museum's *Evolving Planet*. You'll also see gorillas, man-eating lions and best of all, Sue – the largest Tyrannosaurus Rex on the planet. Well, her skeleton anyway. You can go to ancient Egypt, to the snowy land of the Eskimos, or learn about the spirit-gods of the South Pacific. We'd need this whole book to tell you everything, so you just have to go see for yourself. Be sure to get a CityPASS for half-price admission on this and four other cool attractions.

Flag of Chicago: Blue stripes, white stripes and red stars.

The blue stripes are Chicago's great waterways: Lake Michigan and the Chicago River. The white stripes are its neighborhoods, the North, West and South Sides. The first red star remembers Fort Dearborn. The second star mourns the Great Fire of 1871. The third and fourth stars stand for the two great Chicago Expositions (which we love to call the Absolutely Awesome World's Fairs).

Flamingo
Would you have guessed that this is a bird?

That's what Alexander Calder had in mind when he made this 53-foot-tall, 50-ton steel sculpture. Chicago is full of awesome outdoor sculptures. You can see this one in the Federal Plaza, and a real flamingo in the Lincoln Park Zoo.

Flight of Daedalus and Icarus:
A huge glass mosaic.

Over the front door of the 120 North LaSalle Building is a mosaic that tells the ancient Greek story of Daedalus and Icarus, who tried to fly by making wings out of feathers and wax. In the story, Daedalus told his son Icarus not to fly too close to the sun, but he did anyway. The wax melted, and Icarus fell into the sea. So if a grownup tells you not to fly too close to the sun wearing wax and feather wings, it's a good idea to pay attention.

Ford Center for the Performing Arts
Oriental Theatre
Very fancy!

This building with the long name was once a movie theater so glamorous that it had golden statues, and the ushers wore turbans! There were jeweled furnishings from the Far East, and even two golden thrones. Inside, the theater still looks like a royal palace, but now it's one of Chicago's best places to see Broadway shows and concerts.

Fountain of Time
Who are all these people?

That's Father Time standing on one side of this remarkable reflecting pool, as 100 people trudge past him on the opposite side. Father Time is the symbol of life, from newborn to old age. The sculptor, Lorado Taft, made one of the people look just like himself. Can you find him? He's the man with his hands behind his back. The *Fountain of Time* sculpture is in Washington Park on Chicago's South Side.

Fountain of the Great Lakes: An easy way to remember.

A sculptor named Lorado Taft designed an artistic way to remember how the Great Lakes flow. This fountain at the Art Institute of Chicago shows five women pouring water. The woman at the top is Lake Superior, because that's the biggest of the Great Lakes. Its water flows into the others. The other women represent Lake Michigan, Lake Huron, Lake Erie and Lake Ontario. Some people thought it was silly to show women as lakes, but now it is one of Chicago's favorite attractions.

Four Seasons Mosaic

The world-famous Russian/French artist Marc Chagall gave this beautiful mosaic to the City of Chicago. Using only glass and stone, he created six scenes of the city. How many will you recognize? See it at the First National Plaza at Dearborn and Monroe Streets.

Frisbee® Player
He looks alive, doesn't he?

A very famous sculptor named J. Seward Johnson loves to make sculptures that look exactly like real people doing every-day things. *Time Out* almost looks like real people tossing a Frisbee® in the park. Check it out at the Presidential Towers.

Gangsters!

One of America's most famous criminals, Al Capone, caused all sorts of trouble for Chicago in the 1900s. He helped start a crime organization called The Outfit that was involved in gambling, beer and whiskey bootlegging, and murder. Back then, a lot of people called it "The Capone Gang." Al Capone spent several years in prison at Alcatraz. He is buried in Hillside, near Chicago.

Garfield Park Conservatory
Help a bee pollinate a flower.

If you always wanted to climb a giant bean, slide down a vine, or help a giant bee pollinate a giant flower, this is the place. The Garfield Park Conservatory is a huge garden under glass that grows plants all year, even when there's snow outside. Does it look like a big glass haystack to you? Admission is always free. Kids love Wild Wednesdays, when they have all kinds of family adventures, like scavenger hunts and nature projects.

Geocaching: Chicago rocks!

If you're a geocacher, you'll never run out of treasures to find around the cool sites in this book. For those who haven't tried it yet, geocaching is a game where people hide little toys and trinkets in containers that you have to find by using a GPS.

Golden Lady

Some people say this beautiful lady with the flowing robe looks like the Statue of Liberty, even though the Statue of Liberty is four times taller. The Statue of Liberty holds a torch in one hand and a writing tablet in the other. "The Golden Lady," who is covered in real gold, holds a globe with an eagle on top in one hand and a staff in the other. Her official name is *The Republic*, but most people around town think Golden Lady suits her better. See her in Jackson Park and decide for yourself.

Grant Park: Chicago's front yard

This park and its gardens on Lake Michigan are so lovely that people really do call it "Chicago's front yard." It's a great place to see the city skyline. It's hard to believe that before it became a park, this area was a dump. It was filled with debris from buildings burned in the Great Fire of 1871. Now there are pretty bridges and jogging paths, lots of statues and monuments, and the beautiful *Clarence Buckingham Memorial Fountain*, which you already know about. There's also the Art Institute, the Field Museum, and the Shedd Aquarium. In Grant Park you can go ice skating and roller skating, play tennis or miniature golf, or hang out on the lawn for a free music concert. Grant Park is where a million people showed up for President Obama's 2008 election night party.

Great Lakes: The largest group of freshwater lakes on earth.

Chicago sits on the banks of Lake Michigan. Can you name the other lakes? Which is the biggest one?
Hint: Go back to Fountain of the Great Lakes on page 20.

Hint: Go back to Fountain of the Great Lakes on page 20.

Hancock Observatory
You can see forever!

Well, you can see four states anyway. Take America's fastest elevator ride to the observation area on the 94th level of the John Hancock Building. You'll know how Spider-Man must feel climbing up the side of a building. You can even get your picture taken in a trick shot that makes you look braver than Spider-Man. On summer nights, it's also a great place to watch the Navy Pier fireworks.

Heald Square Monument:
Very important hand shaking.

That is definitely George Washington up there, but who are those two men shaking hands with him? Well, it's Mr. Hyam Salomon, a great patriot who raised piles of money to help win the Revolutionary War, and Mr. Robert Morris, the financial leader of the Thirteen Colonies. When you figure out that the money these two men raised is worth about 50 billion dollars today, you would understand why President Washington is shaking their hands. Heald Square is in the Michigan-Wacker Historic District.

Hemingway, Ernest
World-famous fisherman and author:
Born in Chicago.

The author of *The Old Man and the Sea* (and some of the other greatest books of all time) was born in a pretty house on Oak Park Avenue. It is a Queen Anne style house that his grandfather built. When he got older, Ernest was called Papa Hemingway. He lived in many places around the world, including Cuba, Paris (France), and Key West (Florida). But Chicago was his first home.

Hershey's Chicago
Jolly Ranchers in your ears?

Just kidding! Only dumb people would put real candy in their ears, but at Hershey's Chicago store you can get Jolly Rancher earphones, Bubble Yum earphones and even York Peppermint Pattie earphones. Of course you can also get Hershey Kisses and other famous chocolate things to eat – and if you buy something yummy at the bakery, like a cupcake topped with Reese's Pieces, maybe the "Hershey-izer" will sing for you. Did you know there really was a Mr. Hershey? He especially loved Chicago because he discovered chocolate-making machines at Awesome World's Fair #1.

Holocaust Museum: The importance of remembering.

This museum has no dinosaurs or play areas. It's about remembering the saddest and most horrible period in world history, and honoring the people who were killed in the Holocaust. The Illinois Holocaust Museum and Education Center has many outstanding photos and exhibits. There's a real 20th-century German rail car like the ones that took millions of people to the concentration camps. *The Hall of Remembrance* is a youth exhibit especially for 9 to 12 year olds. Even though it is sad, it has an important purpose. People walk into this museum through the "dark side" and come out on the "light side." They want to make sure nothing like this ever happens again, and they feel hope for the future.

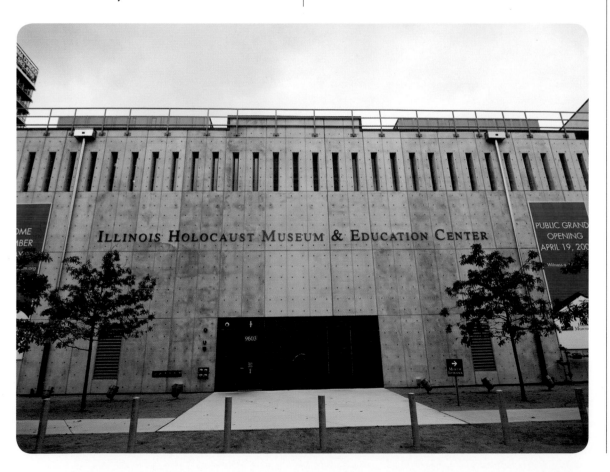

Hot Dog, Chicago Style: No ketchup, ever!

Chicago is famous for many things, but nothing more than its amazing all-beef dog on a poppy seed bun. Load it up with really bright green sweet pickle relish, sliced tomatoes, onions, sport peppers, a deli pickle spear or some cucumber slices, and good ole yellow mustard (but not that fancy Dijon mustard). And never, ever should you put ketchup on a Chicago-style hotdog.

Hyde Park: Malia and Sasha lived here.

Hyde Park is a neighborhood on Chicago's South Side. It's also the name of the huge park where Awesome World's Fair #1 took place. The Obama girls grew up in the Hyde Park neighborhood before they moved to the White House. Nearby are many beautiful mansions, museums and theaters, and the University of Chicago. Hyde Park once was a really tough neighborhood, but the city and businesses worked to make it a great place to visit and live. Hyde Park has bicycle and jogging paths, picnic spots, tons of statues and monuments, and exciting outdoor festivals. Be sure to check out the view of Lake Michigan from Promontory Point.

Ice Skating
Fun and free!

Love to ice skate? Chicago has free outdoor rinks in several parks. The two most impressive are the Olympic-sized rink at Midway Plaisance Park in the Hyde Park neighborhood, and the spectacular rink at Millennium Park. The smaller rinks, like the one at Daley Bicentennial Plaza, may be less crowded.

Illinois and Michigan Canal: 96 miles of scenery.

The Illinois and Michigan canal was cut through beautiful woodlands for boats to get from the Great Lakes to the Mississippi River. When railroads were built, the canal wasn't needed so much. So the National Park Service took it over, and now people can go hiking, camping, kayaking, horseback riding, fishing, snowmobiling, and lots more.

Jackson Park: Playgrounds, beach, golf course and gardens.

Are you in the mood for a picnic or a bike ride? Jackson Park is the perfect spot! The beautiful park was named for President Andrew Jackson. It was designed by the two world-famous landscape architects (Frederick Law Olmsted and Calvert Vaux), who designed New York's Central Park.

Jordan, Michael: The stats.

If you're a serious "Air Jordan" fan, you need to know the stats, so here they are:

Born February 17, 1963. Height: 6'6"; shoe size: 13. Played basketball for the University of North Carolina (Chapel Hill) Tar Heels. Round One draft pick for the Chicago Bulls, 1984; joined the team as a shooting guard. Rookie of the Year, 1985. Six NBA Championships (1991, 1992, 1993, 1996, 1997, 1998). Five-time NBA MVP; six-time NBA Finals MVP, and 14 time NBA All-Star. Olympic Gold Medals, 1984 and 1992. Sports Illustrated Sportsman of the Year, 1991. ESPN "Greatest North American Athlete of the 20th Century," 1999. Inducted into the Basketball Hall of Fame in 2009.

Juicy Fruit Gum: Just for soldiers?

That's true; Chicago's own Wrigley Company makes Juicy Fruit gum (also lots of other chewing gums, plus Skittles and Starbursts). During World War II, they had only enough supplies to make a small amount of gum, so every bit of it went to the United States Armed Forces.

Kohl Children's Museum
Build your own house!

Yes, at the *Hands On House*, you get to design your own house. You pick the materials, build the walls, and put on the roof. Then you can paint it, carpet it, and put bushes in the yard. Would you rather work on cars? You can change tires, fix the engine and even drive through the car wash, and a million other things at the Kohl Children's Museum. Sweet!

Kwanusila: A real totem pole.

What is a 40-foot-tall totem pole, carved by the chief of the indigenous Kwagiulth tribe in Canada, doing in Chicago? The original was a gift to the city from James Kraft, founder of Kraft Foods. It stood here in Lincoln Park for 45 years. It was returned to the tribe in 1985. This one is an exact copy. The base is a sea monster. Above that is a man riding a whale, and on top is a thunderbird, which in the indigenous language is *kwanusila*.

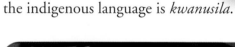

The 'L': Red Line, Brown Line; Pink, Blue and Yellow Line.

And don't forget the green, purple and orange lines! No, it's not a box of crayons – it's the color map that helps people get around Chicago on the 'L' – America's third-busiest rapid transit system. The fast trains have been running north and south, east and west for more than 100 years. Pick up your route map and go!

Lake Michigan
Thanks, Ice Age!

During the Great Ice Age, massive sheets of ice (glaciers) moved across North America, flattening mountains and carving out valleys. They finally melted, making five ginormous lakes. But there was no such word as "ginormous" when the lakes were named, so they're called the Great Lakes. Lake Michigan is the largest body of fresh water in the United States. It has everything for a great vacation: beaches, fishing, sailing, state parks, and wildlife. Chicago is at the southwestern tip of Lake Michigan.

Land of Lincoln: America's 21st state.

The name Illinois comes from the French word for land and the Algonquin word for warrior. So Illinois is the "Land of Warriors." Maybe you can guess that our state slogan is "Land of Lincoln," because it was the home of our 16th president, Abraham Lincoln. But did you know we have two other native presidents? Ulysses S. Grant, #18, and Ronald Reagan, #40 were also born in Illinois. Chicago is the largest city in Illinois.

Legoland®
Not just for kids.

If you didn't already love Legos® before you got to Legoland®, you'll definitely love them by the time you leave. At the Legoland Discovery Center you can ride a dragon made completely of Legos. You can explore a Lego jungle and a Lego castle. You'll see Harry Potter and Batman made of Legos, and even the city of Chicago, made of one and a half million Lego pieces. Then, if you like, you can build your own Lego invention. Legoland is in the Streets of Woodfield Shopping Center.

Lincoln Park Zoo
Gorillas and penguins and bears, oh my!

It started with just two swans more than 100 years ago. Now it is home to more than 1,200 animals from big gorillas to creepy crawlies. At the Pritzker Family Children's Zoo and the Farm-in-the-Zoo, even the smallest guests are invited to feed the cows and meet goats and chickens. The zoo is open year round and it's free.

Lincoln Park: Chicago's biggest.

At more than a thousand acres, this is the largest public park in Chicago's Park District. It was named in memory of President Lincoln. It has gardens, sports fields, a golf course and beach – and best of all, the Lincoln Park Zoo, the Lincoln Park Conservatory, the Peggy Notebaert Nature Museum, and an outdoor stage for summertime performances.

Magnificent Mile: Chicago's glamorous avenue.

Fancy hotels, fine stores, skyscrapers, beautiful trees and flowers, and tons of great restaurants: that's what you'll see along this one mile-long section of Michigan Avenue. With cool places like the Lego store, American Girl Place, Hershey's Chicago, ESPN Zone, and the Chicago Children's Museum, the Magnificent Mile is definitely not just for grownups.

Marshall Field's Clock: Still keeping time.

"The Great Clock" has been hanging there, outside the old Marshall Field & Company's State Street Store, since 1897. The people of Chicago were very proud when the famous artist, Norman Rockwell, did a painting of it in 1945 for the cover of the *Saturday Evening Post*. Marshall Field's is now Macy's, but the beloved clock is still ticking along.

Merchandise Mart
What color is it today?

You can tell what season it is by the colors that light up this huge white building at night. At Halloween it lights up orange; on St. Patrick's Day it's green, and at Christmas it's red and green. "The Mart," which takes up two whole city blocks, is filled with everything it takes to design and furnish a house. Crossing the river in front of The Mart is the famous red Wells Street Bridge.

Mexican Art: Colorful, musical and fun!

Some people call the National Museum of Mexican Art the hidden jewel of Chicago museums. Through its wonderful collection of paintings and textiles, pottery and sculpture, as well as its music and dance performances, you will get to know the Mexican people from earliest history to today. Each spring the museum puts on a free family festival, Dia del Nino, and every Sunday admission is free.

Michigan Avenue Bridge: Connecting the skyscrapers.

Twice a week in springtime, the draw-bridge section in the center of this cool-looking bridge is raised up to let lots of people sail their boats out of storage docks and into Lake Michigan for the summer. Twice a week in autumn, they open again so the sailboats can sail back in to hibernate for the winter. This "sailboat parade" is a very pretty sight. If you absolutely, positively need to know exactly what kind of bridge this is, it's a double-leaf, double-deck, fixed counterweight trunnion bascule. You can stand on the observation deck and watch the giant gears work.

Midwest
What exactly is it?

Chicago is the biggest city in the American Midwest, but what exactly is the Midwest?

It's the middle section of the United States that covers 12 states. How many can you name? Turn the page upside down to see the answers.

Illinois, Indiana, Iowa, Kansas, Michigan, Minnesota, Missouri, Nebraska, North Dakota, Ohio, South Dakota, and Wisconsin.

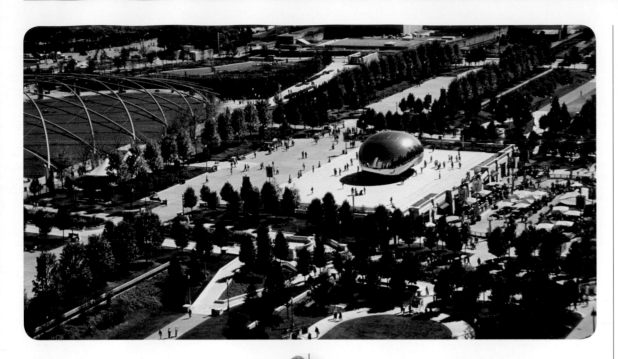

Millennium Park
Just plain gorgeous.

It would be hard to decide what part of Chicago is the most impressive – the skyscrapers, the shoreline of Lake Michigan, or the green spaces – but Millennium Park would be right up there at the top of the list. You've got your Bean (page 7), your Jay Pritzker Pavilion (page 41), your Crown Fountain (page 15), the ice rink (page 26), and the BP Bridge (page 6), plus all those statues and monuments.

Miro Sculpture: The Sun, The Moon, and One Star.

Many of Chicago's sculptures and monuments were made by the most important artists in the history of the world. The City of Chicago paid famous Spanish "surrealist" Joan Miro half a million dollars to make this sculpture when he was almost 90 years old. Nearby is a sculpture by his friend Picasso (you can go to page 6 for a look).

Mummies! (But no daddies)

Do you dare enter the tomb of Unis-Ankh? Have you ever been close to an Egyptian mummy, or traveled down the Nile River? At the Field Museum you can do these things. You'll peek in at everyday life in Ancient Egypt, home of Cleopatra, the mythical Cat Goddess and more! Find out more about the Field Museum on page 18.

Museum Campus
Three-in-one and loads of fun.

If you have only one day in Chicago, Museum Campus would be a great place to spend it. The Shedd Aquarium, the Field Museum, and the Adler Planetarium are all right here on Lake Shore Drive, next to Soldier Field. Get here by car, train or bus, but get here!

Museum of Science and Industry
Interactive to the max.

This museum not only is interactive, it invented interactive! You can test, touch, and experience the most important inventions of the past and things inventors are working on right now that don't even exist yet. Like what? Well, imagine an instant-message hug that you can actually feel! Since it's the largest science museum in the entire Western Hemisphere, there's no way you can do all the experiments, watch all the shows, and see all 35,000 artifacts in one visit. But you can make a good start!

Naper Settlement: A Conestoga wagon, geocaching and more.

Imagine growing up in a pioneer family 175 years ago, riding over mountains and through rivers in your Conestoga wagon to settle in the wilderness of the Midwest. Come see what life was like for the Naper family without running water, electricity, or the Internet. Meet the blacksmith, the stone carver, and other village characters, and check out the replica of Fort Payne, built for protection during the Blackhawk Indian War. Naper Village has a really fun geocaching program, too. The big prize is a Naper medallion.

Navy Pier: What would you like to do today?

You have to plan carefully because there are so many choices! Shall you ride the Ferris Wheel? Take the high speed Transporter FX to the moon? Sail on Lake Michigan aboard the spectacular Tall Ship *Windy*? If you love IMAX movies, Navy Pier has the largest IMAX screen in Chicago. We are not making this up: it is six stories high! The Chicago Children's Museum is here too, and so many restaurants you'll go crazy trying to decide. Have a blast!

Ness, Eliot: Enemy of Al Capone.

Al Capone was one of Chicago's worst "bad guys" ever (remember him from page 22?) The good guys who were always chasing him were United States Treasury agents nicknamed "The Untouchables." Eliot Ness was the leader of The Untouchables. After many years, Eliot Ness finally helped to put Al Capone in jail.

Nobel Peace Prize
President Obama wasn't Chicago's first!

© ® The Nobel Foundation

The first American woman to win the Nobel Peace Prize was Jane Addams, from Chicago. Miss Addams and Ellen Starr Gates were social welfare workers. They started Hull House, to help poor and sick people, especially women, children, and European immigrants. Hull House still carries on the important work they began.

Nuclear Reactor
Chicago and the atom bomb.

The first atomic bomb was tested in the desert of New Mexico, but a lot of the research and testing of the first nuclear reactor took place at the University of Chicago. Before and after World War II, several University of Chicago scientists tried to warn the government about the horrible dangers of using nuclear energy for weapons. This sculpture by Henry Moore sits on the exact spot where the nuclear reactor was built.

O

Obama, Barack: 44th President of the United States.

Barack Obama moved to Chicago after graduating from Harvard Law School. He was first elected to the Illinois Senate, and then to the U.S. Senate, representing Illinois. On election night, 2008, more than 1 million people stood in Grant Park to hear President Obama's victory speech, which began with the words, "Hello, Chicago."

O'Hare International Airport: Second busiest in the world.

More than 200,000 travelers pass through this airport every single day, and that includes a whole lot of kids. So the Chicago Children's Museum created *Kids on the Fly*, which has cool airplane and helicopter models to play on, and even a control tower.

Old Water Tower
It did not save Chicago.

Even though it was built for fire protection, this 154-foot tall water tower could not save the city in The Great Chicago Fire of 1871. But because it was built of concrete and stone, it was one of the only buildings that didn't burn down. Have you ever seen a White Castle restaurant? The founder of White Castle supposedly got the idea for the castle design from this very water tower.

O'Leary's Fire Truck Tours: "Hottest Tour in Town."

When Captain George retired from Engine Company 13, he missed his fire trucks so badly he decided to buy one for himself. So now, everyone can hop aboard a real antique fire engine or chief's truck and let Captain George show you Chicago's most interesting sights. You'll even stop at a fire station or two. Reservations are required, weather permitting.

Oprah!

America's rich and famous TV star, Oprah Winfrey, is from Chicago, and her broadcasting studio is Harpo on West Washington Boulevard. Sometimes Oprah gives huge street parties in Chicago and everybody is invited for free.

Oriental Institute Museum: Mysteries of the Ancient Near East.

The 16-foot-long human-headed winged bull and the 17-foot-tall statue of the Egyptian pharaoh Tutankhamun are worth the trip to this museum. It might get pretty weird, too, because in the Kid's Corner, there's even an exhibit that shows you how they prepared a mummy for the afterlife. The museum has thousands of exhibits about the ancient Near East, which included ancient Egypt, Mesopotamia, Persia, and more.

Palace of Fine Arts

It really does look like a palace from ancient Rome or Greece, doesn't it? That's exactly what the architects wanted when they built the fabulous White City for the Awesome World's Fair #1. Inside the Palace of Fine Arts were 10,000 pieces of American art. More than 27 million people came to see the White City, which was way more magnificent than Oz. Dorothy and her friends Lion, Tin Man, and Scarecrow would be even more amazed at the wonders inside, because it's now the Museum of Science and Industry.

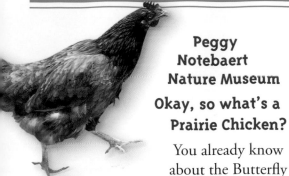

Peggy Notebaert Nature Museum

Okay, so what's a Prairie Chicken?

You already know about the Butterfly Haven (page 9), but many, many other creatures live here, too. Like Beauregard Beaver, Bogart Box Turtle, and Perry Prairie Chicken. Do you like spiders? This museum collection has 200 different kinds, and tons of other stuff, plus craft projects, field trips and sleepovers with the butterflies.

Pillar of Fire
It all started right here.

The people of Chicago believe that this is the exact spot where the Great Fire of 1871 started. Now, instead of a wooden shed at the corner of Dekoven and Jefferson Streets, there's a solid brick building where they train firefighters and police officers. How perfect is that! These bronze flames, called *Pillar of Fire*, remind the firefighters every day of their important mission.

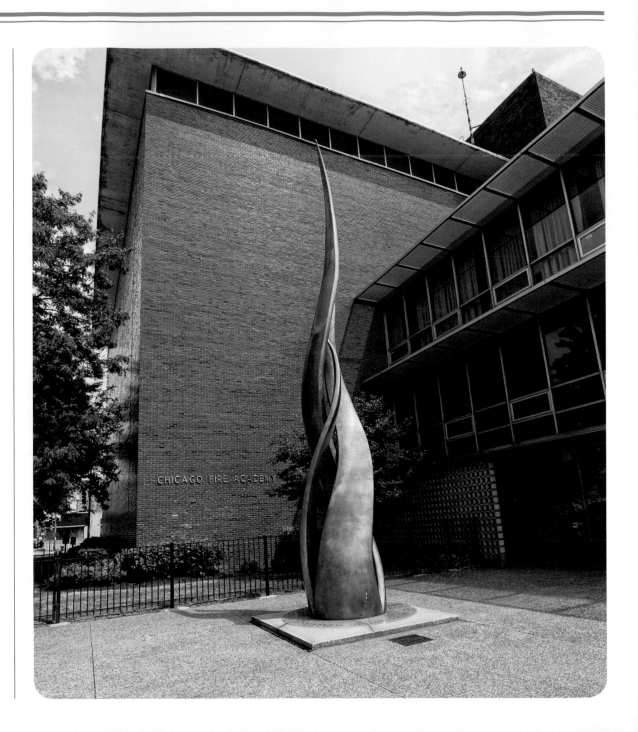

Pizza! Deep dish, Chicago style.

Yes, that yummy deep-dish pizza, with all the cheese and lots of Italian sausage, was invented right here in Chicago. A football star named Ike Sewell came up with the idea at his restaurant called Pizzeria Uno. The restaurant is now called Uno Chicago Grill, and its famous deep dish pizza is still the star of the menu. Want to know the recipe secret? If you promise not to tell anyone, here it is: just mix some cornmeal in with the flour for the dough!

Pritzker Pavilion
Seriously Awesome concerts.

Imagine 11,000 people gathered on this lawn for a concert under the stars. What a party! And the party gets bigger each year during the Grant Park Music Festival, with free concerts all summer long. Do you think the pavilion looks like a giant birthday bow with ribbons of steel?

Q
Questions and Answers

QUESTIONS
find the answers!

- What is the secret ingredient in Chicago Pizza dough? (page 41)

- What never, ever goes on a Chicago style hot dog? (page 25)

- What was the Billy Goat Curse? (page 8)

- Who is the greatest basketball player in history, and what size shoe does he wear? (page 27)

- What bizarre thing happens to the Chicago River once a year? (page 46)

- Where is the biggest Tyrannosaurus Rex skeleton on the planet? (page 18)

- Where can you see a crocodile-headed dinosaur? (page 47)

- Where can you pet a penguin? (page 5)

- What kind of hawks like to play on the ice? (page 8)

ANSWERS
find the questions!

Find the mystery questions in this book!

Page 4
Answer: It was accused of starting the Great Fire of 1871. But it really didn't.

Page 50
Answer: They make half a billion a year!

Page 19
Answer: When a certain bird eats pink shrimp, its feathers turn pink.

Page 13
Answer: Wisconsin, Michigan, Illinois, and Indiana

Page 56
Answer: Southpaw, of course!

Quick Factoids

Betcha didn't know…

Cracker Jacks, hamburgers and other good stuff.

People got their first taste ever, of Aunt Jemima Syrup, Quaker Oats, Cream of Wheat, diet soda, and Shredded Wheat cereal right here in Chicago, at Awesome World's Fair #1. And millions of people went crazy for that strange meat sandwich between two buns: the hamburger!

Garlic? Are you kidding me?

The name "Chicago" came from the Algonquin Indian word meaning "garlic field."

Lincoln Logs

The world's most famous architect, Frank Lloyd Wright (you'll meet him on page 58), had a little boy named John, who grew up to be an architect too. But John was most famous for a very special toy he invented, called Lincoln Logs. Wouldn't he be surprised to learn that, almost 100 years later, kids still love his invention!

Foul Ball!

It used to be against professional baseball rules to let fans keep foul or homerun balls if they caught them in the stands. But Wrigley Field changed the rules and was the first stadium to allow it.

The Loop is not a trick to tie your shoe.

Back when Chicago was a smaller town, The Loop was an actual circle of The 'L' train tracks that ran around the city. Now that Chicago is a big city, The Loop just means "downtown."

River Walk (and cycle too)

When Chicagoans want to remind themselves just what a great city they have, they go for a stroll, or a bicycle ride, or a boat ride along the River Walk. There are restaurants and benches to rest and enjoy the great views of the skyscrapers, bridges, and the Chicago River.

Rookery: A hideaway for pigeons.

The word "rookery" means "nesting place for birds." That's exactly what this grand old building became by accident. Way back in the old days, there were cattle stables nearby, so thousands of pigeons loved nesting in the eaves and hanging out on the roof. When the stables closed down and the building was redesigned with a fancy glass ceiling, the pigeons went away. But people still remember, and they still call it The Rookery. If you happen to be in the neighborhood, look carefully. Can you find the two pigeons carved into the archway?

Rosenberg Fountain
A nice story.

Once upon a time, a little boy was trying to make extra money to help his family by delivering newspapers. When he was thirsty, nobody on his way offered him a drink. "One day," he thought, "I will build a water fountain where anybody can drink even if they have no money." When he grew up, he made lots of money and that's exactly what he did. The fountain is designed to look like a Greek temple. The goddess on the top, holding a pitcher, is Hebe, "cup bearer for the gods." Maybe you would like to have a drink from Mr. Joseph Rosenberg's fountain and think how it would make him smile.

Schooner

You might feel like a Pirate of the Caribbean when you scale the rigging up to the crow's nest of this awesome three-story schooner at the Chicago Children's Museum. Grownups can climb too. It's called The Kovler Family Schooner after the very generous family who have contributed much to the city. Find out more about the Chicago Children's Museum on page 12.

Shedd Aquarium
Tots on Tuesdays.

Hey, if you're age 2, 3, 4 or 5, Tuesday is your most special day at the Shedd Aquarium. Of course, every other day is terrific too. Check out Aquarium on page 5.

Skyscraper: Does it really scrape the sky?

Of course not, but it sure looks that way from the ground! Back 125 years ago, most buildings were no more than two or three stories tall. An engineer named William Jenny realized that a "skeleton" of steel could hold up many more stories. His first skyscraper was only ten stories tall! Now, Chicago has tons of skyscrapers, some are ten times that high! How tall do you think skyscrapers might be 125 years from now?

Soldier Field: Smaller and smaller.

This stadium was named to honor Americans who died in wars. Instead of getting bigger and bigger, this stadium got smaller on purpose, so the fans could get closer to their football team, the Chicago Bears. It is now the smallest stadium in the National Football League.

Southpaw: Mascot of the Chicago White Sox.

In baseball terms, a southpaw is a left-handed pitcher. This Southpaw is left-handed, and also green and furry. Some fans say it's a sock. What kind of creature is that? If you're planning to go to a game and ask ahead of time, maybe Southpaw will come visit you at your seat!

Spider Dan: A real life Spider-Man.

In 1981, a rock climber named Dan Goodwin made himself a Spider-Man costume and scaled the Willis Tower, just like the movie character Spider-Man. Back then, it was called the Sears Tower, and it was the tallest building on Earth. He braved dangerous wind and slippery glass to make the climb in 7 hours. He got in big trouble with the fire department. He wrote a book called *Skyscraperman*, explaining why he climbs tall buildings.

Spirit of Music and SummerDance.

For thirty-three nights and ten Sunday afternoons each summer, the Spirit of Music Garden in Grant Park is filled with music and dance. More than 40 different kinds of bands perform on stage, from African beat to square dances and swing. There are free lessons and anyone can get up and dance. The beautiful statue is called *Spirit of Music*.

St. Patrick's Day
Chicago River turns green.

Each year, on the Saturday before St. Patrick's Day, almost half a million people (most of them wearing green) line up to see the parade up Columbus Drive and to check out the Chicago River, which "magically" turns a bright Irish green.

Standing Lincoln
In Lincoln Park.

Chicago is famous for its hundreds of public monuments, statues, and memorials. One of the oldest is this statue of President Abraham Lincoln about to give a speech. You can tell that he has just gotten up from his chair, and you almost feel that in any second you will hear his voice.

Suchomimus: A crocodile-headed dinosaur.

If you were tromping around in the swamp during the Cretaceous period (more than 100 million years ago), the last creature you would want to meet would be, a huge, spiky crocodile-headed dinosaur with ginormous claws. And it would be even worse if you were a fish, because you would have been his dinner! The Suchomimus bones were discovered in deepest Africa by a famous Chicago dinosaur hunter, Dr. Paul Sereno. Now kids can go on a dinosaur hunt and dig up Suchomimus bones at the Chicago Children's Museum. You might even see Dr. Sereno himself, because he teaches at the University of Chicago!

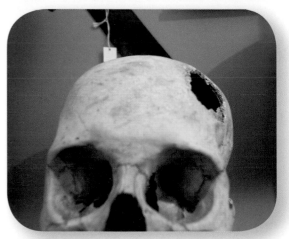

Sundial at the Planetarium

This important looking bronze sculpture in front of the Adler Planetarium and Astronomy Museum is both a work of art and a real sundial. It looks like the bow part of a bow and arrow, doesn't it? Its scientific name is "bowstring equatorial sundial." The sculptor, Henry Moore, named it *Man Enters the Cosmos* because the year he made it, we were just starting to send satellites into space. Read the instructions at the base, and then see if you can tell what time it is by the shadow it casts.

Surgical Museum
Future doctors, check this out!

The International Museum of Surgical Science is totally awesome, even if you don't plan to be a brain surgeon in the future. It has more than 7,000 objects showing how they performed operations from primitive days to today. How did they do surgery on battlefields? What does the body look like without its skin? Have you ever seen an artificial heart? You can even see the death mask of that powerful warrior and emperor, Napoleon.

The Trib: The Chicago Tribune newspaper.

With its spires and gargoyles, this spectacular skyscraper looks more like a French cathedral than a newspaper office. And wait till you hear about the rocks. The builders stuck rocks from all over the world into its limestone wall. There are fragments from Abraham Lincoln's home, the Parthenon in Athens, Greece; the Coliseum in Rome, Italy; the old Berlin Wall, the Alamo, the Great Wall of China, and the Taj Mahal in India. There's also a piece of rock from every state in the United States and every continent, and even a moon rock on loan from NASA.

Trolley Ride

A fun way to get around to many of the fun and tasty places in this book is the Chicago Trolley and Double Decker Company's Hop On Hop Off tour. Some of the stops are Chicago's famous Garrett Popcorn store, the Shedd Aquarium, the Adler Planetarium, the John Hancock Observatory, the Michigan Avenue Bridge. Take as long as you want at each stop, then hop back on!

Trump Tower
Really, really, really tall.

This is a brand new hotel and condominium tower built by gazillionaire Donald Trump. The fun thing about this building is that it looks like a different shape from each side. The tower was going to be 150 stories tall, but after September 11, Trump decided to make it only 96. Still, it will be the tallest residential building in the world.

Trunnion Bascule?
Why, it's a seesaw bridge, of course!

Though it looks sort of like a roller coaster, the Cortland Street Bridge was built more than 100 years ago to rise up and let big boats through. It's called a trunnion bascule bridge, and it was the first one ever built in the United States. Now there are more than 35 of them crossing the Chicago River, which makes this city the "movable bridge capital of the world."

Twinkies®
Started with Banana Cream

Before your grandparents were born, a Chicago area company called Hostess Bakery made the first Twinkie®. It was filled with banana cream. But during World War II, they had a very hard time getting bananas, so they switched to vanilla-flavored cream. How many Twinkies® do they make every year? You will have to look at the second **Answer** on page 42 to find out.

U.S. Cellular Field: White Sox home field.

You'll say "Take me out to the ball game" when you find out about this stadium's way-cool kids' section called Comcast Fundamentals. (*FUN*-damentals, get it?) There are baseball clinics, batting cages, practice base running and pitching areas. You have to wear regular athletic shoes (no Crocs or flip flops) to play. On really hot days, you can cool off in the misty Rain Room near section 107 and 537.

U-505: World War II German submarine.

The United States Navy captured this German submarine, lurking deep in the Atlantic Ocean, on June 4th, 1944. It was full of top-secret military information that helped America and the Allies during World War II. The submarine was going to be destroyed, but the people of Chicago raised the money to buy it, and gave it to the Museum of Science and Industry.

Union Station
Wow, this is a REAL train station!

Like several other Chicago buildings, this place looks more like a palace than a train station. The Great Hall has a pink marble floor and 18 Greek columns. And just look up at that atrium! No wonder some people call Union Station one of the greatest indoor spaces in the United States.

United Center: Blackhawks and Bulls.

What kinds of creatures are Blackhawks and Bulls? You can find the answer on pages 8 and 9. But here's a clue: United Center, where they hang out, is the largest sports arena in the U.S. Besides sports, it's the perfect place to see big concerts and shows like the Ringling Brothers and Barnum & Bailey Circus, and Disney on Ice.

Universities

There are four really big universities and several smaller ones here. They have more than 100,000 students and 75 sports teams in all. If you go to DePaul University you're a Blue Demon. If you go to Northwestern University you're a Wildcat. The University of Chicago has the Maroons; and the University of Illinois, Chicago has the Flames. Can you guess where they got the idea for the name, "Flames?" Right! The Great Chicago Fire!

Urbs in Horto
Urbs in whato???

The official motto of Chicago is *Urbs in horto*. That's Latin for "city in a garden." This makes perfect sense, doesn't it, for a city with 552 parks and thousands more acres of parklands?

Venetian Night: A seriously sparkly boat parade.

Everybody loves a parade! This one is on the water at night, with twinkly lights and music. First, there's a magical procession of boats along Lake Michigan, and then there's a huge, spectacular fireworks show. And… you get to stay up past your bedtime!

Victory Monument: African American soldiers.

This statue stands in the section of Chicago's South Side named Bronzeville. It honors African American National Guardsmen who served with the Eighth Regiment during World War II. Bronzeville, which is also called Black Metropolis, has been a very important neighborhood in Chicago's African American history.

Vietnam Veterans Memorial: 2,900 names.

People come from all over the United States to find the names of their friends, brothers, sisters, parents, aunts, uncles, cousins, and grandparents, that are listed on the Vietnam Veterans Memorial. These brave people died for their country and some were missing in action. Visit the memorial at Wacker Drive and State Street.

W Washington Park: Lawnmower sheep?

This large park in Bronzeville has many playgrounds and sports areas, and also summertime festivals. A hundred years ago, they didn't have big rider mowers to keep the lawns trimmed, so they let sheep graze on the grass. The DuSable Museum of African American History is here in Washington Park, and so is that cool *Fountain of Time* sculpture that you saw on page 20. Can you guess which United States president this park was named after?

Water Taxi
Like a bus, but loads more fun.

For just a couple of dollars, kids can hop aboard a boat called a water taxi to get to cool places like museums, the Ferris Wheel at the Navy Pier, Chinatown, the parks, and festivals. Grownups pay a little more, but not much more. You can also take a water taxi tour, where a guide points out lots of the places found in this book. Of course, it's much too cold to do this in winter, so the water taxis start in the spring and end in the fall.

Waterfowl Lagoon
One-legged flamingos?

Don't feel sorry for all the pretty pink birds that look like they have only one leg. They just like to keep the other one tucked up under their body to stay warm. You can see flamingoes, swans, and geese on the Waterfowl Lagoon in the Lincoln Park Zoo. Why are flamingos pink, anyway? Take a guess and see if you're right on page 42.

WaterWays
Splash, get wet, be a scientist.

If you always wondered how they made the crazy Crown Fountain on page 15, or the beautiful Buckingham fountain on page 13, *WaterWays* at the Chicago Children's Museum is your kind of place. Oh yes, you will get wet, when you splash, squirt, and work with different kinds of water systems like water wheels, pumps, and fountains. You even get to try out locks like the ones that raise and lower the water level in Lake Michigan. Better bring along an extra t-shirt to change into afterward!

White City
Half a billion dollars!

That's how much it cost to build the dream city of the future for Chicago's Awesome World's Fair #1. Just as everything was emerald green in the "Emerald City" in the movie, *The Wizard of Oz*, these buildings were all covered in white plaster and painted white.

White Sox: World
Series champs.

Most cities in the United States have no major league baseball teams at all, so Chicago fans feel pretty special to have two. The White Sox are the South Siders, and the Cubs (on page 15) are the North Siders. The White Sox colors are black, white, and silver. Do you remember the mascot's name? (Hint: it's on page 45). The team used to be called the White Stockings. That was a pretty good name back 100 years ago, when people called socks "stockings." But now we call them socks, so now they are the White Sox.

Willis Tower Skydeck
Do you dare stand out there?

If you were brave enough to stand on the observation deck at the 94th level of the John Hancock Building (page 23), you are now ready to graduate to the Willis Tower. It used to be called the Sears Tower. It is the tallest building in the United States and has the highest observation deck in the Western Hemisphere. In the elevator are huge flat screen monitors that make you feel like you're blasting right into space. Your speed will be 1600 feet per minute! When you step into one of the glass boxes on the 103rd floor, the people on the sidewalk below will look like ants, and the cars will look like toys!

Windy City: Chicago's nickname.

Chicago is not even one of the windiest cities in the United States, but that's what people have been calling the city for more than a century.

World's Columbian Exposition

Which Awesome World's Fair was this? What color was the city? What was the famous fair ride? Flip back to page 4 to find out!

Wright, Frank Lloyd: Great American architect.

"What? A house with no basement and no attic? No paint? Windows in the roof? Glass walls? What a crazy architect!" That's what people said when Frank Lloyd Wright moved to Chicago and started designing strange houses. But it turned out that people loved his work and paid him lots of money to design many buildings in Chicago and around the world. The Robie House in this picture is one of his designs. You can take the Design Detectives Family Tour of his home near Chicago.

Wonderland Express: Trains, gingerbread houses, and more.

Every year, right after Thanksgiving, the Chicago Botanic Garden in Glencoe turns into a magical holiday place. There are gingerbread houses, decorated trees, ice-skating, and snowshoeing. A miniature train runs all around the tracks. You can have breakfast or supper with Santa, or hot chocolate with Mrs. Claus. The Wonderland Express is only 20 miles from Chicago, which is about 3,400 miles closer than the North Pole!

Wrigley: The chewing gum people.

Actually, Mr. Wrigley didn't invent chewing gum. He was a soap salesman who had the great idea to give away a stick of gum to anybody who bought his soap. Then he decided to make his own gum instead of buying it from somebody else. Today, it takes farmland bigger than 30,000 football fields to grow all the mint they need to make their mint-flavored gums! This beautiful white skyscraper is Wrigley's world headquarters.

Wrigley Field: Home of the Cubs.

This is the second oldest ballpark in Major League Baseball. (Boston's Fenway Park is the oldest.) It was named for the chewing gum Wrigleys, who owned the field and the Cubs too. Check out the flag waving from center field after a game. If it's a blue W, the Cubs won the game. If it's a white L, the Cubs lost.

X Braces: Monster arms.

People are always asking, "What are those humongous X's on the outside of the John Hancock Building?" If you would like to be the smart one who knows the answer, here it is: They are monster-size steel "arms" crossing the building to make it stronger against powerful winds.

Yellow Popcorn. Really, really yellow!

Why are people happy to wait in line for popcorn? You'll know why when you taste Chicago's famous Garrett Popcorn. It does come plain or buttered if you really want it that way, but the real treats are the melt-in-your-mouth, oh, so cheesy CheeseCorn, and the light-as-air, sweet CaramelCrisp. Pick your favorite and they'll make it fresh, right before your eyes, in a big copper kettle. You can even get it with pecans, cashews, or macadamia nuts.

Yummy! Taste of Chicago.

Three million people show up every summer for the world's largest food festival. Taste of Chicago is a ten-day summer festival to show off the food from Chicago's amazing restaurants. But it's a whole lot more than just food. There's face painting, live music, movies, games, and performances on many stages.

Zephyr
Wanna drive this train?

This shiny silver train is nicknamed "Silver Streak." Its real name was the Pioneer Zephyr. It's an antique now, of course, but at Awesome World's Fair #2 it was the most modern train people had every seen. Now it lives at the Museum of Science and Industry. You can climb aboard and look around, and even take the controls – just like an engineer.

Zoo!

Oops, you don't want to miss this! Go back to page 30 and find out where it is. See you there!

Index

My Trip to Chicago

Date:

Stuff we did:

Been There, Done That!

sticker sheet

Now that you've seen the historic monuments, learned all the interesting facts, and visited the fun attractions of Chicago, it's time to mark where you've been and what you've done. Simply match the places on the stickers to their correct location on the map to create your own personal guide around Chicago.

Adlar Planetarium

BP Pedestrian Bridge

Buckingham Fountain

Chicago Children's Museum

Field Museum of Natural History

Grant Park

Hancock Observatory

Lincoln Park Zoo

Merchandise Mart

Millenium Park

Museum of Science and Industry

Navy Pier

Shedd Aquarium

Water Tower

Willis Tower

Wrigley Building

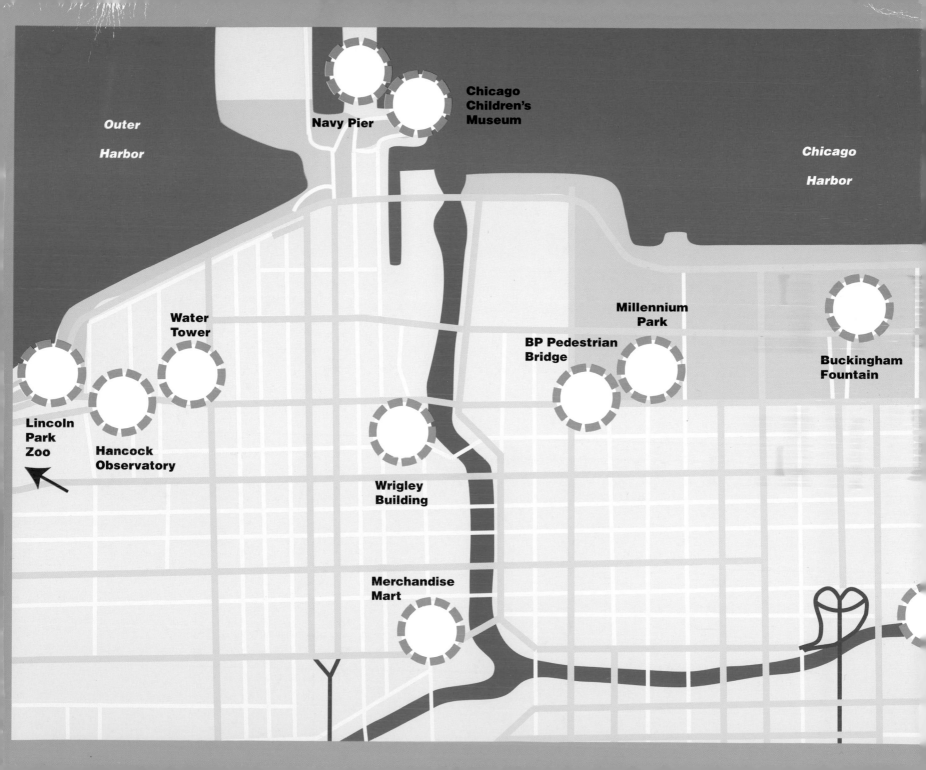

Lake

Michigan

**Adlar
Planetarium**

*Burnham
Park
Harbor*

**Shedd
Aquarium**

**Museum of
Science and
Industry**

**Grant
Park**

**Field Museum of
Natural History**

**Willis
Tower**

A KIDS GUIDE TO
Chicago